Key Stage LEARN

How Things Happen & The Natural World

NAPE National Association for Primary Education

Contents

AUTHOR: Camilla de la Bédoyère
EDITORIAL: Catherine de la Bédoyère, Quentin de la Bédoyère, John Bolt, Vicky Garrard, Kate Lawson, Sally MacGill, Julia Rolf, Lyndall Willis
DESIGN: Jen Bishop, Dave Jones, Colin Rudderham
ILLUSTRATORS: David Benham, Sarah Wimperis
PRODUCTION: Chris Herbert, Claire Walker
Thanks also to Robert Walster

COMMISSIONING EDITOR: Polly Willis
PUBLISHER AND CREATIVE DIRECTOR: Nick Wells

3 Book Pack ISBN 1-84451-050-6 Book ISBN 1-84451-017-4
6 Book Pack ISBN 1-84451-065-4 Book ISBN 1-84451-078-6
First published in 2003

A copy of the CIP data for this book is available from the British Library upon request.

Created and produced by
FLAME TREE PUBLISHING
Crabtree Hall,
Crabtree Lane,
Fulham, London SW6 6TY
United Kingdom
www.flametreepublishing.com

Flame Tree Publishing is part of The Foundry Creative Media Co. Ltd.

Printed in Croatia

Foreword

Sometimes when I am crossing the playground on my way to visit a primary school I pass young children playing at schools. There is always a stern authoritarian little teacher at the front laying down the law to the unruly group of children in the pretend class. This puzzles me a little because the school I am visiting is very far from being like the children's play. Where do they get this Victorian view of what school is like? Perhaps it's handed down from generation to generation through the genes. Certainly they don't get it from their primary school. Teachers today are more often found alongside their pupils, who are learning by actually doing things for themselves, rather than merely listening and obeying instructions.

Busy children, interested and involved in their classroom reflect what we know about how they learn. Of course they learn from teachers but most of all they learn from their experience of life and their life is spent both in and out of school. Indeed, if we compare the impact upon children of even the finest schools and teachers, we find that three or four times as great an impact is made by the reality of children's lives outside the school. That reality has the parent at the all important centre. No adult can have so much impact, for good or ill, as the young child's mother or father.

This book, and others in the series, are founded on the sure belief that the great majority of parents want to help their children grow and learn and that teachers are keen to support them. The days when parents were kept at arm's length from schools are long gone and over the years we have moved well beyond the white line painted on the playground across which no parent must pass without an appointment. Now parents move freely in and out of schools and very often are found in the classrooms backing up the teachers. Both sides of the partnership know how important it is that children should be challenged and stimulated both in and out of school.

Perhaps the most vital part of this book is where parents and children are encouraged to develop activities beyond those offered on the page. The more the children explore and use the ideas and techniques we want them to learn, the more they will make new knowledge of their very own. It's not just getting the right answer, it's growing as a person through gaining skill in action and not only in books. The best way to learn is to live.

I remember reading a story to a group of nine year old boys. The story was about soldiers and of course the boys, bloodthirsty as ever, were hanging on my every word. I came to the word khaki and I asked the group "What colour is khaki?" One boy was quick to answer. "Silver" he said, "It's silver." "Silver? I queried. "Yes," he said with absolute confidence, "silver, my Dad's car key is silver." Now I reckon I'm a pretty good teller of stories to children but when it came down to it, all my dramatic reading of a gripping story gave way immediately to the power of the boy's experience of life. That meant so much more to him, as it does to all children.

JOHN COE
General Secretary
National Association for Primary Education (NAPE).

NAPE was founded 23 years ago with the aim of improving the quality of teaching and learning in primary schools. The association brings together parents and teachers in partnership.

NAPE, Moulton College, Moulton, Northampton, NN3 7RR, Telephone: 01604 647 646 Web: www. nape.org.uk

How Things Happen & The Natural World is one of six books in the **Learn Series** for Key Stage One. These books have been devised to help you support your child as they begin Primary School.

This book introduces you and your child to the science topics covered in Key Stage One. You should go through the book together; your child will need you on hand to guide them through each subject. There are both written and practical activities throughout the book which will help reinforce the concepts that are covered.

You will also find **Parents Start Here** boxes to give you extra information and guidance.

Before you begin any learning session with the book, ensure your child is relaxed and comfortable:

- They should be sitting with their feet touching the floor and their bottom at the back of their seat.
- Put the book at a slight angle so your child can see their pencil point as they write.
- Encourage a good writing grip; good habits are as easy to develop as bad ones.
- Give your child access to water; research suggests that children who drink water when they work perform better.

Do not attempt to complete too many pages in one sitting; children have short attention spans and you want the experience to remain pleasurable. Offer your child plenty of praise for the work they accomplish. Reinforce the learning with lots of activities away from the book – science is primarily a practical subject and children can explore and discover many scientific principles themselves.

If your child struggles at any point put the book down, take a break and think about other ways you can teach an idea or concept. Use of alternative media, such as television programmes, newspapers, the Internet and CD-ROMs can help to bring topics alive and give them relevancy.

There is a checklist at the end of the book; you can use this to show your child how they are progressing. You could introduce a reward system too; children benefit enormously from rewards and praise.

Most importantly, the time you spend together with this book should be enjoyable for both of you.

Parents Start Here...

Help your child think about the differences between living and non-living things before they progress to the next page.

Is It Alive?

It may be easy to tell if some thing is alive ...

... or it may not!

These are things that are alive:

Things that are alive are either animals or plants.

These are things that were once alive, but now are dead:

These are things that have never been alive – they are non-living:

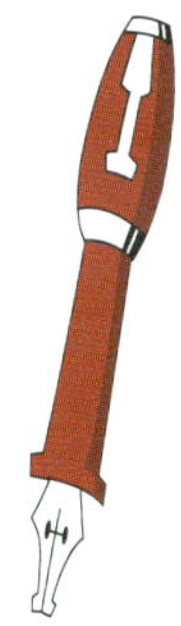

Home Learn

Draw a circle around the things that are alive:

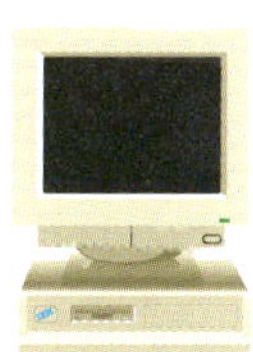

TRY THIS

Activity

All living things grow – can you think of anything else that all living things do?

Check Your Progress!

Is It Alive? ☐

Turn to page 48 and put a tick next to what you have just learned.

Parents Start Here...

Talk to your child about when they were a baby and show them photographs so they can see how much they have grown and changed.

It's Alive Because...

There are 7 things that all living things do (and that means all plants and animals):

Grow

Plants grow from seeds. Humans and other animals grow from being babies into adults.

Move

You cannot see plants move but they do; they move their leaves towards the sunlight. Even animals that are stuck to rocks, like barnacles, move. You just might not see them!

Feel Things

We can feel, see and hear. Plants can 'feel' the sunlight, and move towards it.

Breathe

We breathe air with our lungs. Plants breathe air through their leaves.

Have Babies

We have babies, dogs have puppies and plants have seeds!

Feed

Animals find food and eat it.
Plants make their own food using sunlight.

Get Rid Of Waste

You go to the toilet to get rid of the waste your body has made. Plants breathe out their waste into the air.

Home Learn

Join the fathers to their babies. One has been done for you.

Activity

Draw pictures of your three favourite animals.
Think about how they move, grow and have babies.

Check Your Progress!
It's Alive Because... ☐

Turn to page 48 and put a tick next to what you have just learned.

Top Tip!
Remember to give your child lots of praise – they'll work so much better.

Parents Start Here...

Recognising similarities and differences in living organisms is the first step in understanding how living things are classified and may have evolved – subjects your child will cover in future years.

What Is An Animal?

What is the difference between animals and plants?

Animals eat food and they can move from one place to another. Plants make food in their leaves and they usually stay in one place.

These are all animals – but they look very different from one another.

Some of these animals have 2 legs, some of them have more and some of them have no legs at all! Can you think of any other differences?

We may look very different to a slug, but there are some animals we are very similar to, such as chimpanzees.

We both have legs to walk with

We both have faces with eyes, ears, noses and mouths

We both have hands, with fingers and thumbs

We both have fur (human fur is called 'hair')

We both have families

Home Learn

Write:

the name of one animal that has 4 legs ________________

the name of an animal that has scales ________________

the name of an animal that roars ____________________

TRY THIS

Activity

Play a game of Animal Consequences with a friend. You both fold a piece of paper up, then unfold the first 5 cm and draw an animal head on it. Fold this bit of paper over then swap with your friend. (Keep your drawings secret). Draw the middle part of an animal, roll again and swap. Draw the animals' bottom bits. Unroll the paper and see the amazing animals you've created.

Check Your Progress!
What Is An Animal? ☐

Turn to page 48 and put a tick next to what you have just learned.

Top Tip!
If your child loses concentration here, let them take a break.

Parents Start Here...

There is increasing awareness in schools of the importance of teaching children good lifestyle habits – but the best examples are set at home; it's up to you.

Move It!

Animals move in lots of different ways.

They can swim

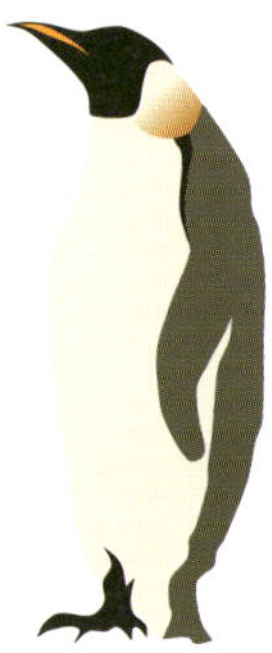

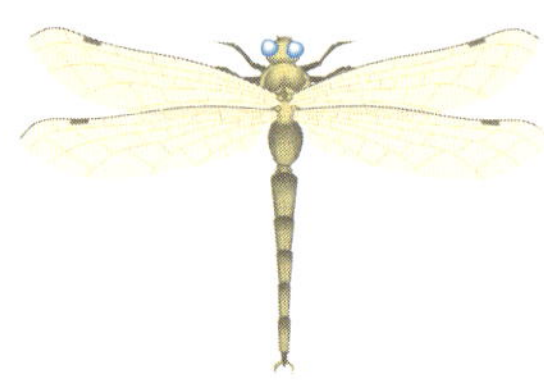

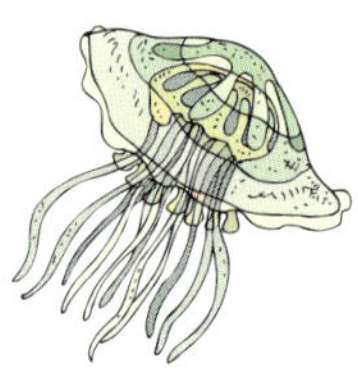

They can fly

They can climb

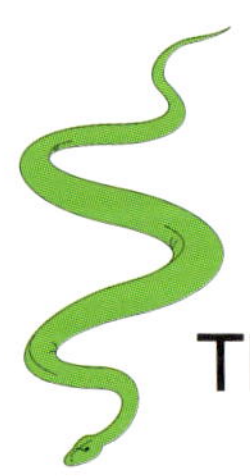

They can slither

They can jump

They can walk

Can you think of any other ways that animals move?

How do **you** move around?

Moving around is good for you. **Running, jumping, skipping, climbing** and **playing outside** are all great ways to build muscles and bones. This keeps your body fit and strong.

Make sure you play outside or do some exercise every day of your life.

Home Learn

Tick ✓ the activities you think are good exercise:

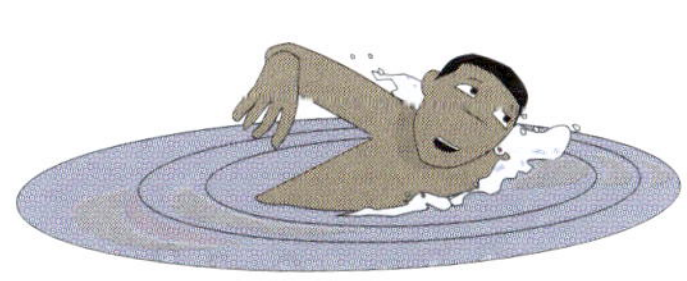

TRY THIS

Activity

Pretend to be an animal moving around. Can everyone guess what you are trying to be?

Check Your Progress!

Move It!

Turn to page 48 and put a tick next to what you have just learned.

Parents Start Here...

As your child learns more about nutrition you can let them get involved in planning the family's meals.

Food And Drink

All animals need food to eat and water to drink. Food and water give animals the energy to move and grow.

These animals only eat plants

These animals only eat other animals

These animals eat both plants and animals

This cow has to eat grass all day to get enough energy to stay alive.

This snake only has to eat once a year to get enough energy to stay alive.

Humans eat food from plants and animals. We need to eat lots of different types of food to stay healthy and have energy. We also need to drink plenty of water every day, throughout the day.

Humans eat:

Meat, fish and eggs – to build muscles and help our brains grow.

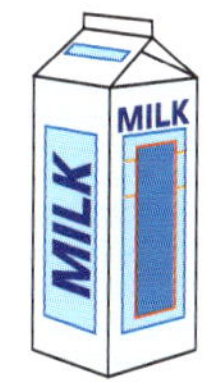

Milk, cheese and butter – to build bones and teeth.

Fruit and vegetables – for our skin, hair and nails, and to keep our bodies free of disease.

Potatoes, rice, bread and cereal – for energy and to keep the insides of our bodies healthy.

Lots of good food, like fruit, contains natural sugar so we do not need any extra sugar. There is sugar in sweets, fizzy drinks, cakes and chocolate. There is loads of sugar in chocolate- and honey-coated breakfast cereals.

Home Learn

Circle the foods you should avoid:

TRY THIS

Activity

If you love sugary foods, try and find other things to eat that are just as yummy, but not so harmful.

Check Your Progress!

Food And Drink

Turn to page 48 and put a tick next to what you have just learned.

Parents Start Here...

This topic provides you with an opportunity to talk about death with your child – it is, after all, the natural consequence of ageing and growth.

Growing

This elephant has not always been huge – it had to grow this big.

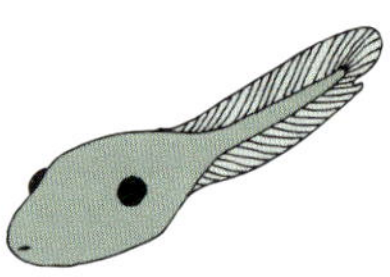

This frog grew from a tadpole. Its parents did not look after it.

This cat has kittens. At first, they are blind and can not look after themselves. The mother looks after them while they grow bigger and stronger.

This caterpillar will soon wrap itself up into a cocoon where it will grow and change into a butterfly.

You have grown a lot since you were born, but you have a lot more growing to do.

Human babies need their mothers to feed them and they need to be looked after for many years. During this time they grow – their bodies change and so do their brains. All this learning is helping your brain to grow bigger and better!

Grown-ups carry on growing too – they may not get any taller (although you may have noticed that they quite often get fatter!) but their skin, hair and nails still grow.

Home Learn

Match the baby to the mother:

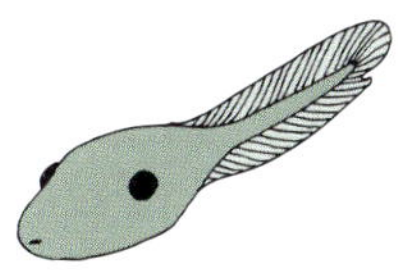

TRY THIS

Activity

Draw around your hands and feet on a piece of paper. Get members of your family and friends to do the same. Paint the hand and footprints then cut them out. Compare the sizes of cut-outs, then use them to make a colourful collage.

Check Your Progress!

Growing ☐

Turn to page 48 and put a tick next to what you have just learned.

Parents Start Here...

The Activity on this page offers your child a chance to observe and record – essential skills in science. When possible, find other opportunities for your child to exercise these skills.

Seeing And Hearing

This owl has very big eyes at the front of its head. It can see well at night, when it hunts.

This mole can not see very well. He doesn't need to because he spends most of his time underground.

This hare has big ears and very good hearing. He needs to listen for foxes which might be hunting for him.

This fish doesn't have any ears. There is not much to listen to under the sea. He can feel movement in the water though, and his eyesight is very good.

If you don't already know where your eyes and ears are – now is the time to find them!

Your eyes are on the front of your head so you can see where you are going. They have eyelashes and tears to protect them from dirt. You must take care of your eyes – they are very delicate and can easily get damaged.

Your ears are on the side of your head. This means you can hear things happening ahead of you and behind you.

Home Learn

Match the ears and the eyes to the animals.

TRY THIS

Activity

Find out the eye colour of all the members of your family, including uncles, aunts and cousins if you can, and record your results in a chart like this:

	Me	Mum	Dad	Tom	Liz
eye colour	green	blue	green	brown	brown

Check Your Progress!

Seeing And Hearing ☐

Turn to page 48 and put a tick next to what you have just learned.

Parents Start Here...

Set out saucers of similar-looking food ingredients and let your child taste the differences (e.g. cornflour, salt, bicarbonate of soda, sugar).

Smelling, Tasting And Touching

Noses are very useful:

- they warm and clean the air as we breathe it in
- they help us to smell things. If something smells bad we know we must not eat it.

Tongues are very useful:

- they help us to talk and eat
- they taste things and this means we can enjoy our food.

Skin is very useful:

- it helps protect our bodies from disease
- it can feel things. If we touch something hot we know we must move our hand away from it.

We have seen that animals (including humans) can:

- **See things**
- **Hear things**
- **Smell things**
- **Taste things**
- **Touch things**

These are the five senses and they help us learn about the world we live in so we can keep ourselves safe, find food and look after others.

Home Learn

Which senses would you use to tell the difference between:

A piece of glass and a piece of ice ______________________

A cup of tea and a cup of vinegar ______________________

A rose and a daffodil ______________________

A guitar and a piano ______________________

TRY THIS

Activity

Close your eyes when you eat and think about the flavours of the food. Can you describe the taste using words like 'salty', 'sweet' and 'sour'?

Check Your Progress!

Smelling, Tasting And Touching

Turn to page 48 and put a tick next to what you have just learned.

Parents Start Here...

Choosing and buying vegetables offers a good opportunity to talk about plant structure with your child. It may even encourage them to eat vegetables with more enthusiasm!

Plants

Plants come in many shapes and sizes ...

tree | flower | rose | carrot | cactus | water lily

... but most of them have leaves, roots, a stem and flowers.

Colour in this picture of a plant.

Flowers attract insects to the plants. They help to make the seeds.

Leaves turn sunlight into food.

The stem holds the plant upright.

Roots help keep the plant in the ground and collect water from the soil.

This apple tree has lots of leaves and its roots go far underground. The flowers (we call them 'blossom') come out in spring. The stem is called a 'trunk'.

This cactus has a big, fat stem that stores water. The spikes on the cactus are tiny leaves. This plant produces only one or two flowers a year.

This is a pine tree. Its leaves are long and thin – we call them 'needles'. This tree never flowers but it does have pine cones.

Home Learn

Match the part of the plant that we eat with the vegetable:

lettuce **carrot** **broccoli** **celery**

stem **leaves** **root** **flowers**

TRY THIS

Activity

Get a saucer of water and a piece of paper towel. Put one drop of food colouring in to the saucer and stir. Now dip the corner of the paper towel into the water and wait. The way water moves up the towel is similar to the way water moves through a root and into a plant.

Check Your Progress!

Plants ☐

Turn to page 48 and put a tick next to what you have just learned.

Parents Start Here...

This experiment will show your child that light brings about a change in the leaf (you know, of course, that this is photosynthesis) and will help them see how important light is.

How Plants Live

Plants need water to live. There is water in the soil and this moves into the plant's roots.

Plants need sunlight to live. They use the light to make their own food.

Some special plants even eat food, rather like animals.

This plant is called a Venus Flytrap. It catches flies in its leaves then turns them into a gooey liquid, which it uses for food.

We need vitamins in our food to help us keep healthy – plants are the same. The soil contains goodness that the plants can use to grow stronger. That is why farmers put fertiliser into the ground and we give 'plant food' to pot plants.

Home Learn

Put the missing words into this sentence:

died water sunlight dark

I gave my plant some __________ and I put it in the cupboard. The plant went yellow and did not look healthy. I think it was too __________ in the cupboard. Then I put the plant in the __________ but I did not give it any water. After two weeks my plant had wilted and __________.

TRY THIS

Activity

Use a paper clip and a piece of tin foil to cover up half of a leaf on a living plant. Keep it in the light and water it as normal. After two weeks take the tin foil off and look at the leaf.

Check Your Progress!

How Plants Live ☐

Turn to page 48 and put a tick next to what you have just learned.

Parents Start Here...

Unless it is summer or autumn your child may have trouble finding seeds outside. Buy some fruits for them to examine and get books from the library.

The Life Cycle Of A Plant

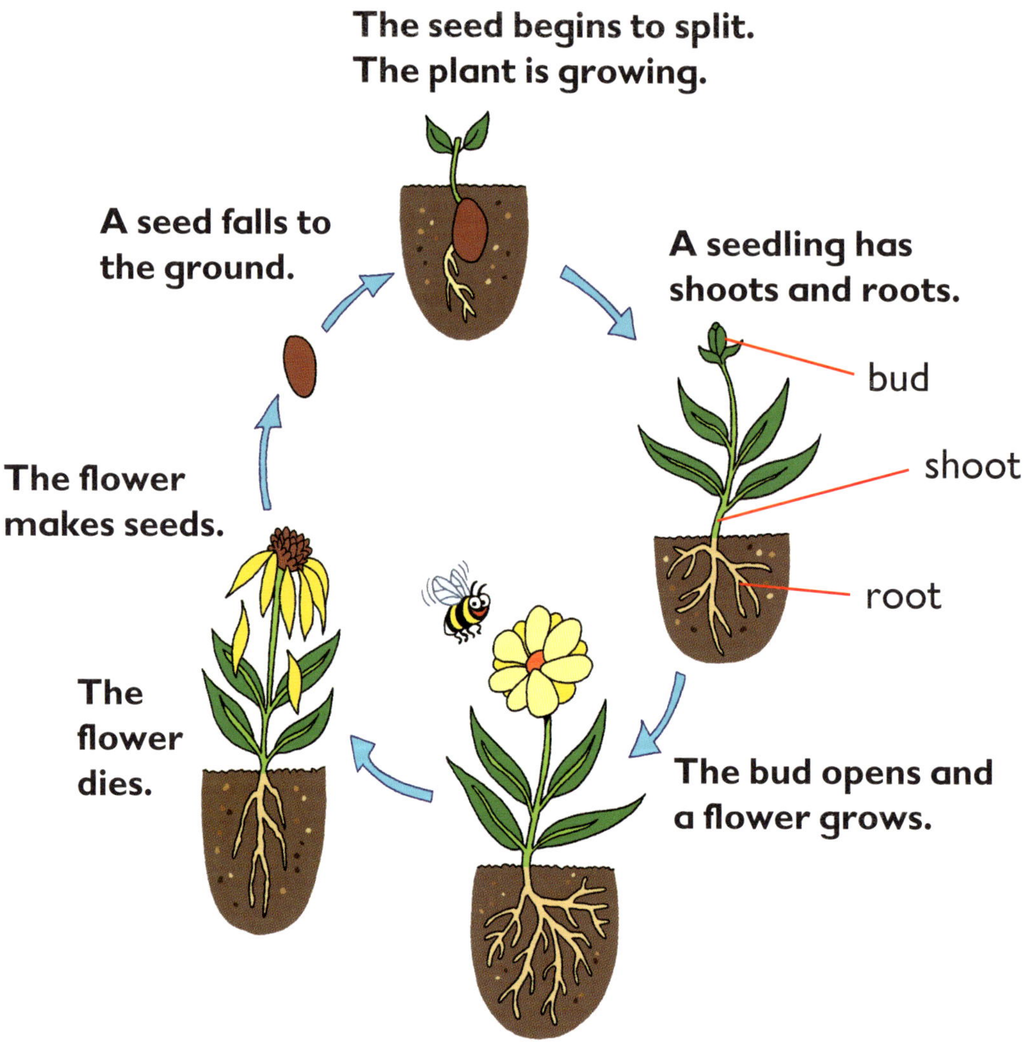

Plants make seeds so that new plants can grow. Seeds often have hard shells outside to protect them during the winter. Think of an orange pip or a peach stone; they are both very hard.

Seeds travel from where they were made to where they will grow.

Dandelion seeds are very light so they float away in the wind.

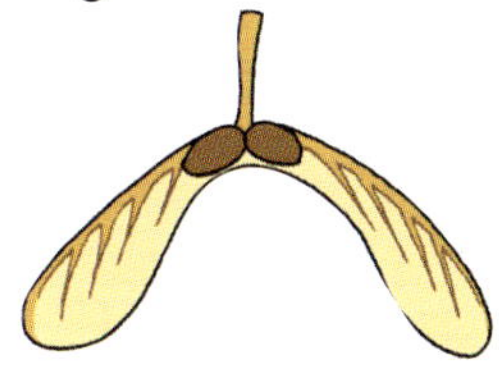

Sycamore keys are seeds. They are a good shape for flying in the wind.

Some seeds are hidden inside juicy fruits so they get carried away by animals that eat them. Strawberries have their seeds on the outside of the fruit.

Pea pods explode when they dry out in the hot days of late summer. The peas, which are seeds, get flung across the ground.

Home Learn

Match the word to its meaning:

root	a) Attracts insects.
flower	b) Keeps it stuck in the ground.
leaf	c) Travels to start a new plant growing.
seed	d) Is green and makes food for the plant.

Activity

Look at the plants in your garden or local park and think about what type of seeds they have and how those seeds travel. Draw the seeds.

Check Your Progress!

The Life Cycle Of A Plant ☐

Turn to page 48 and put a tick next to what you have just learned.

Parents Start Here...

Children often focus on the larger, more appealing animals, but the minibeasts offer a fascinating insight into animal life, and they are much more accessible to a child than polar bears and crocodiles!

Minibeasts

We have looked at plants, animals and humans and we have learned a lot about how they all live. There is a HUGE group of animals we have not talked about yet – the minibeasts.

The minibeasts are the small animals, smaller than your hand. Here are some minibeasts:

Some interesting facts about minibeasts:

- There are lots more minibeasts in the world than all the other animals put together.
- Insects are minibeasts that have 6 legs.
- Spiders have 8 legs and are not insects.
- There are over one million types of insect on this planet.
- Leeches are worms that suck blood.
- There are fossils from minibeasts that were made over one billion years ago!
- Some minibeasts carry diseases. Mosquitoes carry malaria, which kills millions of people every year.

Minibeasts matter because:

- Insects help plants to make seeds. Without their help we wouldn't have any more plants – so no more food for us and other animals.
- Minibeasts in the sea are food for the fish that we eat.
- Some minibeasts, like flies, carry diseases but other minibeasts, like spiders, kill the flies.

- They are the food for many animals, like birds.
- Bees are minibeasts that make honey.
- Minibeasts make the ground fertile. This means that plants can grow there. If there were no minibeasts there would be no jungles, parks, woodlands or farms. That means no food for anyone!

Home Learn

Match the minibeast to its name:

spider butterfly worm bluebottle bee ladybird snail

TRY THIS

Activity

Carefully lift a few rocks in the park or garden and look underneath. There will be lots of minibeasts for you to watch. Put the rocks back carefully without harming the minibeasts.

Check Your Progress!

Minibeasts ☐

Turn to page 48 and put a tick next to what you have just learned.

Top Tip! If your child loses concentration here, let them take a break.

Parents Start Here...

Children rarely think about what happens to rubbish after it has been thrown away. Help them investigate this subject at your local library.

Living Together

These animals and plants live together in a desert, which is a hot and dry place. They can survive without much water.

These animals and plants live together in a jungle, where it is hot and wet. There is lots of food in a jungle so many animals can live here.

These animals and plants live under the sea, where it is very wet! Not much sunshine can get through the seawater so there are not many plants living here.

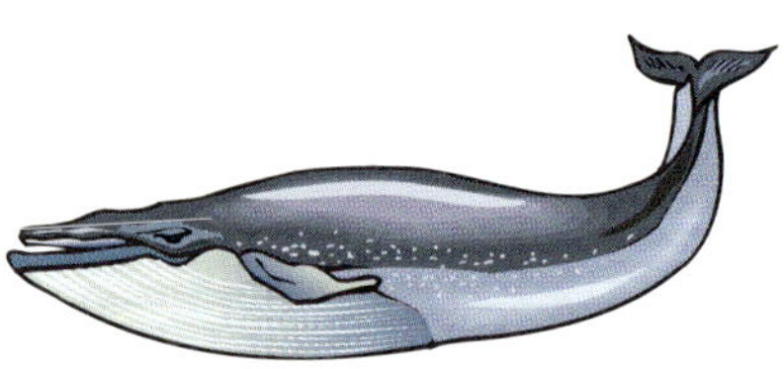

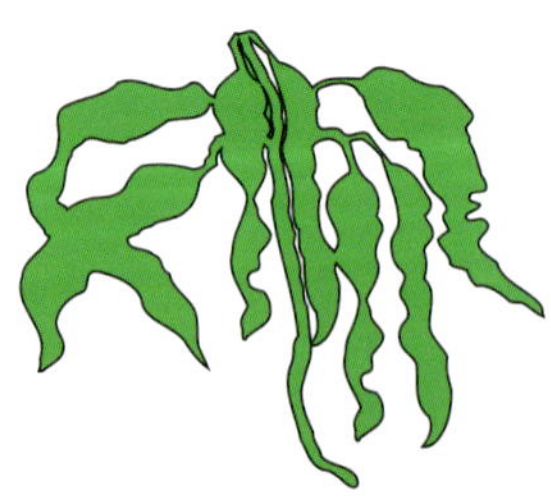

People live all over the world, in hot, cold or warm countries. We have to look after the places we live in, not just for us, but for the animals and plants we live with.

We can keep the world as a good place to live in by:

- **Putting litter in bins.**

  Litter is harmful for little animals and children.

- **Recycling.**

  Paper comes from trees that have been cut down. If we recycle our paper, fewer trees have to die.

- **Cutting down on waste.**

  Try not to buy things that are wrapped in lots of plastic which just gets thrown away. All our rubbish gets dumped in the sea or put in the ground – where it stays for thousands of years.

Home Learn

Circle the things that can be recycled.

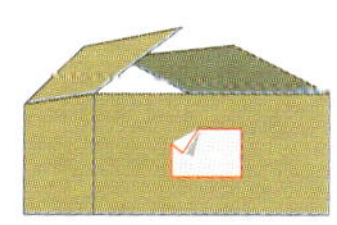

TRY THIS

Activity

Ask a grown up to help you find out what things can be recycled in your area. Are there things you throw away that you could be recycling?

Check Your Progress!

Living Together ☐

Turn to page 48 and put a tick next to what you have just learned.

Parents Start Here...

Talk to your child about other natural materials, such as cork, silk and linen and where they come from.

Materials: Natural

The word material describes what things are made of.
There are many types of material. An object may be made from more than one type of material.

Look at your shoes.
What materials are they made of?

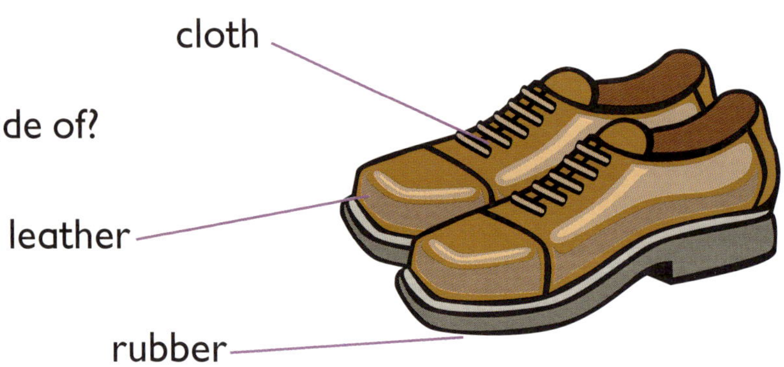

Rubber is used for the sole of your shoe because it is bouncy. This means you can walk a long way without getting sore legs. Rubber comes from rubber trees.

Leather is used for most of your shoe because it is strong and changes shape to fit your foot. It stops water from getting to your foot (unless you get your shoes very wet). Leather is made from cow skin.

Cloth, or fabric, is used for the laces because it is strong and can change shape. Cloth is made from plants.

Rubber, leather and cloth are all natural materials because they come from animals, plants or the ground.

Other natural materials are:

Wool – comes from sheep fur

Paper and wood – come from trees

Bricks and clay – come from the ground

Metal and precious stones – come from rocks

Home Learn

Match the material to what it comes from:

cow

sheep

rocks

oak tree

bricks

leather

wood

wool

TRY THIS

Activity

A pearl is like a precious stone – but it doesn't come from rocks. Find out where a pearl comes from.

Check Your Progress!

Materials: Natural ☐

Turn to page 48 and put a tick next to what you have just learned.

Parents Start Here...

Before moving on to the next topic ask your child to think of reasons why plastic is such a useful material (e.g. waterproof, bendy, strong, can be coloured or see-through etc). This will help them to start thinking about properties of materials.

Materials: Man-Made

When cavemen took a bath they used a pond.
Now we can sit in plastic baths.

Plastic is a material that has been made in a factory.
No one had invented plastic when cavemen were around.

We call plastic a man-made material.

Plastic is a useful material and you probably have lots of it in your house:

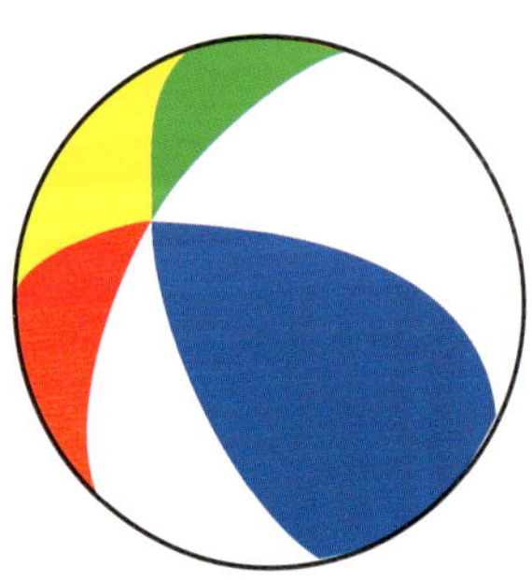

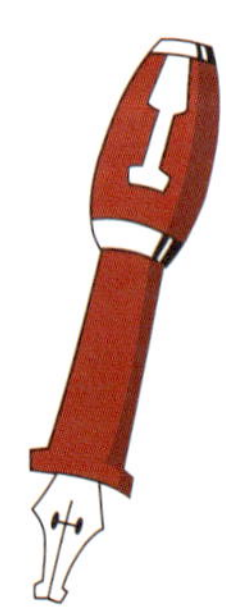

Nylon and polyester are also man-made materials that you may have heard of. They were invented by scientists and are made by machines in factories.

Nylon and polyester are often used to make clothes, sheets or duvets. They feel quite like cotton but they do not need to be ironed.

Think about this:

Man-made materials are made from natural materials.

Sand is a natural material. It is taken to a factory where it gets heated. This changes it to a new material; glass. Oil is another natural material. It is changed in a factory until it becomes plastic.

Home Learn

Put a ✓ next to the objects made from man-made materials.

Rubber tyre

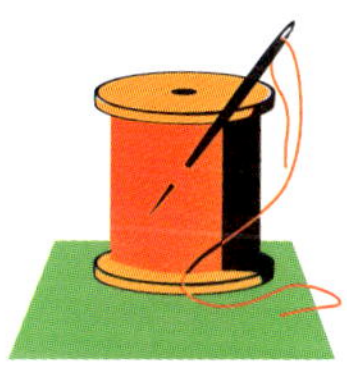
Cotton thread

Glass jug

Nylon stocking

Wool

Wooden chair

Plastic chair

TRY THIS

Activity

Find as many different materials in your house as you can. Decide whether they are man-made or natural.

Check Your Progress!
Materials: Man-Made ☐

Turn to page 48 and put a tick next to what you have just learned.

Parents Start Here...

Conduct an experiment with your child to discover which household objects float, and which don't. Draw up a table together to record your results.

More About Materials

Find a spoon like this one and ask yourself these questions.

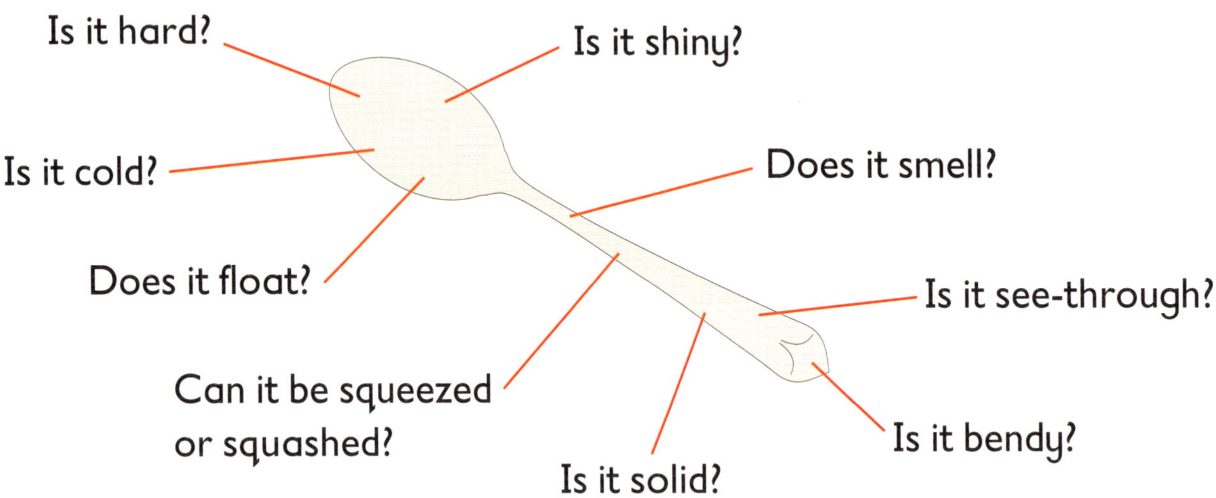

There are lots of words you can use to describe a spoon. These are its properties.

This glass is see-through 

 This mug is not see-through

These plums are soft and you can squash them 

This brick is hard and you cannot squash it 

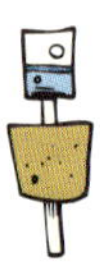 This cork floats

These stones do not float 

When you decide to make something you need to choose a material with the right properties.

When the three little pigs made their houses, only one pig chose a material that was strong enough to keep the wolf away.

If cars were made of cotton, and towels were made of metal – they would not be very good at their jobs!

Home Learn

Draw a line from the word to the right sentence:

hard **see-through** **soft**

a) A knife is made from metal because metal is ___________.

b) A window is made from glass because glass is ___________.

c) Mattresses are filled with feathers because feathers are ___________.

TRY THIS

Activity

You can see through some things that don't look see-through, if you shine a torch at them. Experiment with a torch and paper, a plastic bag, cardboard, a glass of squash or milk etc.

Check Your Progress!
More About Materials ☐

Turn to page 48 and put a tick next to what you have just learned.

Parents Start Here...

This page continues the topic of materials and their properties. On pages 32-33 you asked your child to talk about plastic. Repeat the question, but now your child will have better ways to describe the properties of plastic.

Changing Shape

If this ladder was bendy it would not be very safe.

There are lots of materials that bend and they can be useful (but not for making ladders!).

Some bendy things still have their shape, even after you squeeze, squash, pull or bend them. They are elastic.

catapult

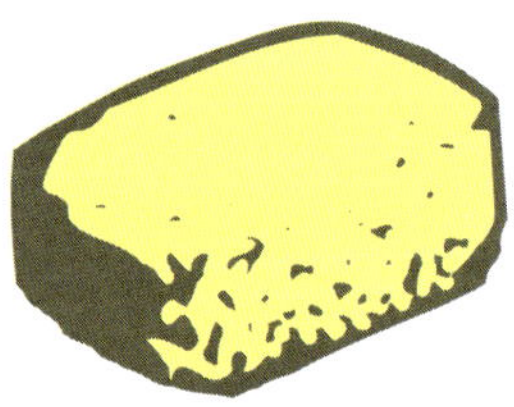

sponge

pencil rubber

Some bendy things can be put into a new shape, and they stay that way unless you bend them into a different shape.

coat hanger

hose pipe

wire

Some things have a shape. They are called solids.

Some things do not have a shape themselves – they just follow the shape of whatever they are put into. They are called liquids.

This jug is full of water. If the water is poured into the glass it will become the shape of the glass rather than the shape of the jug.

Water is a liquid. This means it can be poured.

This balloon is full of air. Air does not have a shape either – it is only this shape because the rubber balloon is making it this shape.

Air is a gas. This means it is very light, it spreads out and does not have its own shape.

Home Learn

Put a tick ✓ next to the things that can be bent, squashed or stretched.

brick

spring

book

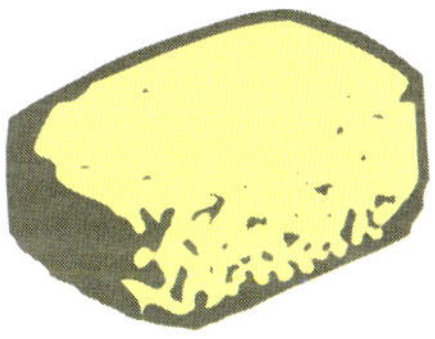

sponge

wooden spoon

catapult

TRY THIS

Activity

You have just learned that water is a liquid, but you also know it can be a solid. Put some water in a plastic container (without a lid) and put it into the freezer for a few hours. What do you get?

Check Your Progress!

Changing Shape ☐

Turn to page 48 and put a tick next to what you have just learned.

Parents Start Here...

After your child has tried the Activity on this page you can explain to them that the water has turned into a gas and gone into the air, and that the salt, which had dissolved, has been left behind.

Heating And Cooling

Some materials change when they get hotter or cooler.

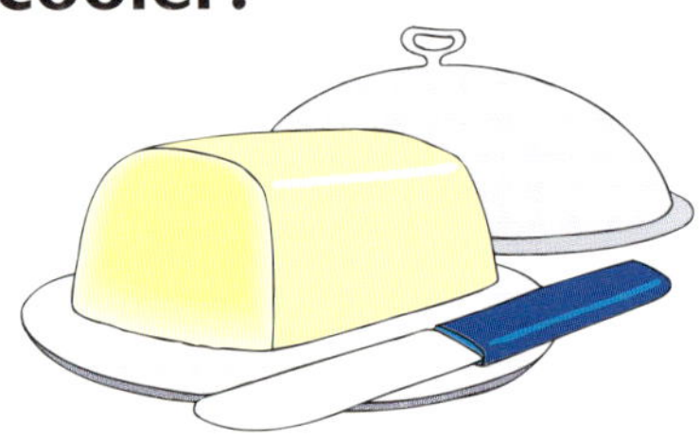

Butter is hard to spread when you take it out of the fridge: it is hard. When it has got warmer it spreads more easily.

Chocolate can melt in a warm hand – it gets soft and squidgy.

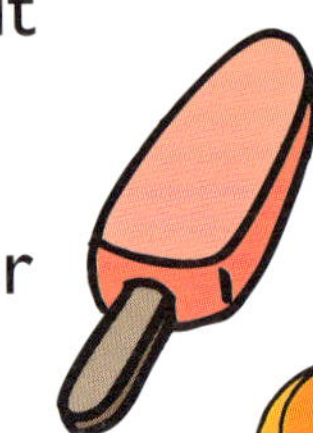

This ice lolly has just come out of the freezer and it is solid.

This ice lolly has been warming up in the sun for a little while. Some of the ice has changed to liquid.

When solid things turn into a liquid we say they have melted. Even very hard things, like rocks, can melt if they get hot enough.

Deep beneath this volcano the rocks have got so hot they have melted and turned to lava.

Have you noticed that on a very hot day the surfaces of the roads get sticky? They are beginning to melt.

You have put some water into the freezer and you saw that it turned into a solid.

You learned that water is normally a liquid, but when you cool it down it freezes to become a solid. We call this solid ice.

When it is very cold the water in the clouds turns to ice.

When the ice warms up it melts to become a liquid again.

We can also turn water into a gas. The next time a grown-up boils the kettle look at what comes out of the spout.

When you heat water it becomes a gas which we call steam. Do not touch steam – it will burn you.

Steam comes out of the kettle.

Home Learn

Put a ✓ next to the things that are solid and a ✗ next to the things that are liquid. Remember that you can pour a liquid.

milk

oil

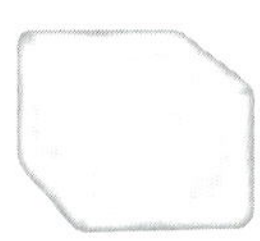

ice

gravy

cake

chocolate

TRY THIS

Activity

Mix some salt and warm water together until the salt disappears. Pour into a saucer and leave in a hot place for a day or two. What happens?

Check Your Progress!

Heating And Cooling

Turn to page 48 and put a tick next to what you have just learned.

Parents Start Here...

Pushing and pulling are just two of the forces your child will eventually learn about. They will also cover friction, air and water resistance, magnetic and gravitational forces.

Making Things Move

When we were learning about animals we discovered that they can move around in different ways, using their legs to walk, run or jump. Some animals move by flying and others swim. Things that are not alive can not move by themselves, but they can be made to move.

You can make this toy car move by pushing it or pulling it.

push

pull

If you push something, you make it move away from you.

If you pull something, you make it move towards you.

A push and a pull are types of force.

If you are pushing or pulling something heavy you need to use a bigger force.

A force can be used to start something moving, or stop it from moving.

push

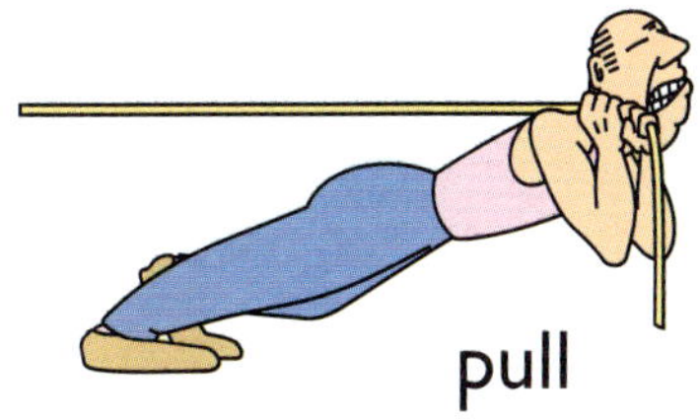

pull

A force can make something move faster or can slow it down.

Home Learn

Put a ✓ next to the things that are being pulled and a ✗ next to the things that are being pushed.

TRY THIS

Activity

Line up all of your toys with wheels and practise pushing and pulling. Notice that the harder you push or pull, the further the toys will move. Do you find that heavier toys are harder to push or pull?

Check Your Progress!

Making Things Move

Turn to page 48 and put a tick next to what you have just learned.

Parents Start Here...

If the sun is shining you can take your child outside to show them the shadows that are being cast. If it is too dark or cloudy, use a torch or small electric lamp indoors to create shadows.

Light

Never look at the Sun because it will hurt your eyes, and damage them forever.

You can see light with your eyes. When you can not see any light everything is dark.

The Sun is a great big burning ball of gases that gives out lots of light.

When you are in your house or at school sunlight comes through the windows but sometimes that is not enough light – so we use electric lights.

Electric lights are not as bright as the Sun but without them we would not be able to see very much once the Sun has set. Never mess around or play with electricity – it can kill you.

Torches are also electric lights, but they get the electricity they need from batteries rather than from electrical sockets in the wall.

Candles and matches can give out small amounts of light. You must never use candles or matches or lighters because they cause fire. Fire can kill you.

Televisions give out light too.

When light is blocked, a shadow is made.

When the Sun is high in the sky a shadow will be short.

When the Sun is low in the sky a shadow will be long

Home Learn

Draw a ring around the things that give out light.

TRY THIS

Activity

On a sunny morning ask someone to draw around your shadow in chalk. Then ask them to do the same thing at noon and in the late afternoon. What do you notice about your shadows?

Check Your Progress!

Light ☐

Turn to page 48 and put a tick next to what you have just learned.

Parents Start Here...

There are plenty of other ways to make music (and noise) at home than are described in the Activity. It's up to you how far you can bear to help your child explore this topic!

Sound

You can hear sound with your ears. There is sound all around us. When there is no sound we say there is silence.

Lots of animals can make sound:

you can sing or talk using your voice

a whale makes a noise only other whales can hear

lions roar to one another

bees buzz

some birds sing, other birds squawk

These things are not alive, but they can all make sound:

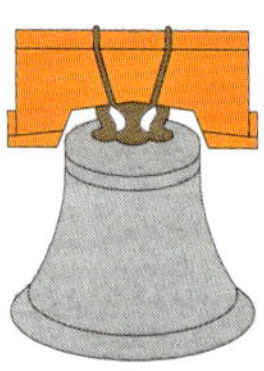

Bell

Alarm clock

Television

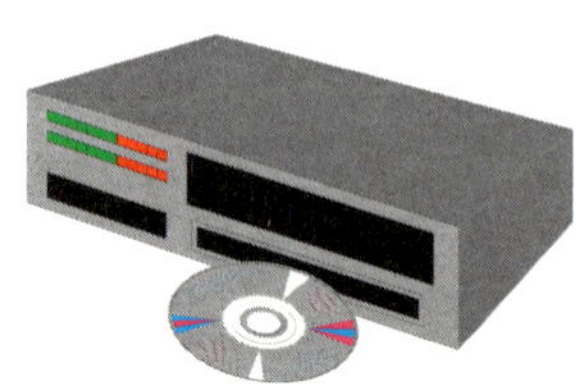

CD player

Musical instruments make sound when we play them:

drums can be banged

pianos and guitars have strings that make the sound

maracas can be shaken

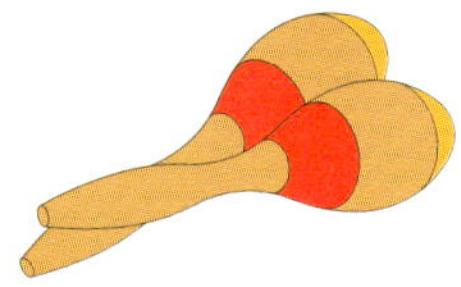
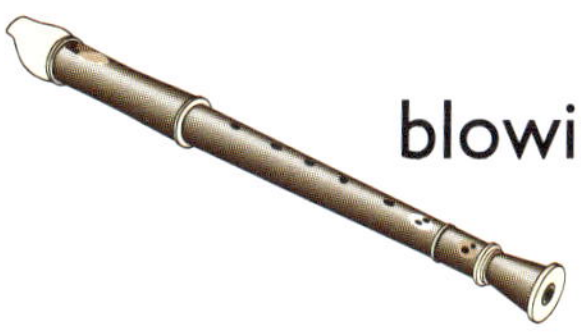

blowing into some instruments will make sound

When musical instruments make sounds they make different notes. Putting certain notes together makes a nice noise – music.

Home Learn

The boy is playing the recorder. Who can hear him loudest? Put a tick in the box.

TRY THIS

Activity

Make your own musical instruments. Line up several bottles and fill with them with water, then blow across the top of the bottles. Try this with different amounts of water. What difference does this make?

Check Your Progress!

Sound

Turn to page 48 and put a tick next to what you have just learned.

Word Search

Find the following words in this word search

Light	Seeing	Teeth	Live	Nylon	Melt
Hot	Sound	Seed	Vegetable	Solid	Soft
Push	Petal	Force	Eat	Eyes	Shadow
Swim	Baby	Taste	Water	Wool	Root

L	I	V	E		W	F			P
S	I	E	A	T	S	O	F	T	E
W	E	G		A		R	O	O	T
I	A	E	H	S	S	C		L	A
M	B	T	D	T	O	E		S	L
N	E	A	E	E	U	L	L	H	T
	Y	B	B	R	N		I	A	E
M	E	L	T	Y	D			D	E
	S	E	O	P	U	S	H	O	T
S	E	E	I	N	G			W	H

Answers

Page 5

Home Learn

The chick and pot plant are both alive.

Page 7

Home Learn

Page 9

Home Learn

a) Some examples: horse, goat, antelope, frog, lizard, pig, mouse etc.

b) Most fish have scales: cod, herring, mackerel, trout, pike etc.

c) Some examples: lion, tiger, bear, panther, leopard etc.

Page 11

Home Learn

Swimming and cycling are both good types of exercise.

Page 13

Home Learn

These are the foods you should avoid:

Chocolate bar

Fizzy pop

Boiled sweets

Page 15

Home Learn

Page 17

Home Learn

Page 19

Home Learn

a) You could use your sense of touch to tell the difference between a piece of glass and a piece of ice.

b) You could use your senses of taste or smell to tell the difference between a cup of tea and a cup of vinegar.

c) You could use your senses of touch, sight and smell to tell the difference between a rose and a daffodil.

d) You could use your senses of touch, sight and hearing to tell the difference between a guitar and a piano.

Page 21

Home Learn

lettuce	leaves
carrot	root
broccoli	flowers
celery	stem

Page 23

Home Learn

I gave my plant some water and I put it in the cupboard. The plant went yellow and did not look healthy. I think it was too dark in the cupboard. Then I put the plant in the sunlight but I did not give it any water. After two weeks my plant had wilted and died.

Page 25

Home Learn

a) Flower – Attracts insects.

b) Root – Keeps the plant stuck in the ground.

c) Seed – Travels to start a new plant growing.

d) Leaf – Is green and makes food for the plant.

Page 27

Home Learn

bee bluebottle butterfly worm

ladybird snail spider

Page 29

Home Learn

All of these things can be recycled.

Page 31

cow	leather
sheep	wool
rocks	bricks
oak tree	wood

Page 33

Home Learn

Nylon stocking

Plastic chair

Page 35

Home Learn

a) A knife is made from metal because metal is hard.

b) A window is made from glass because glass is see-through.

c) Mattresses are filled with feathers because feathers are soft.

Page 37

Home Learn

The things that can be bent, squashed or stretched are: the spring, catapult and sponge.

Page 39

Home Learn

Liquids: milk, oil, gravy.

Solids: ice, cake, bar of chocolate.

Page 41

Home Learn

The supermarket trolley and toy car are both being pushed.

The carriage and the child are both being pulled.

Page 43

Home Learn

The television, sun and candle all give out light.

Page 45

Home Learn

Ally can hear the recorder loudest.

Page 46

L	I	V	E		W	F			P
S	I	E	A	T	S	O	F	T	E
W	E	G		A		R	O	O	T
I	A	E	H	S	S	C		L	A
M	B	T	D	T	O	E		S	L
N	E	A	E	E	U	L	L	H	T
	Y	B	B	R	N		I	A	E
M	E	L	T	Y	D			D	E
	S	E	O	P	U	S	H	O	T
S	E	E	I	N	G			W	H

Check Your Progress

Is It Alive? .... ☐

It's Alive Because . . . . ☐

What Is An Animal? .... ☐

Move It! .... ☐

Food And Drink .... ☐

Growing .... ☐

Seeing And Hearing .... ☐

Smelling, Tasting And Touching .... ☐

Plants .... ☐

How Plants Live .... ☐

The Life Cycle Of A Plant .... ☐

Minibeasts .... ☐

Living Together .... ☐

Materials: Natural .... ☐

Materials: Man-Made .... ☐

More About Materials .... ☐

Changing Shape .... ☐

Heating And Cooling .... ☐

Making Things Move .... ☐

Light .... ☐

Sound .... ☐